The Library of the Thirteen Colonies and the Lost Colony™

The Colony of Pennsylvania

Susan Whitehurst

The Rosen Publishing Group's
PowerKids Press™
New York

For hfc

Published in 2000 by The Rosen Publishing Group, Inc.
29 East 21st Street, New York, NY 10010

Photo Credits: Cover and title page, pp. 5, 7, 8, 12, 15, 16, 19, 22 © Super Stock; pp. 12, 20 © Art Resource; pp. 4, 11 © Bridgeman Art Library; pp. 9, 18 © North Wind Pictures.

First Edition

Book Design: Andrea Levy

Whitehurst, Susan.
    The Colony of Pennsylvania / by Susan Whitehurst—1st ed.
        p.   cm. — (The library of the thirteen colonies and the Lost Colony)
    Includes index.
    Summary: Relates the history of the colony of Pennsylvania from its founding by William Penn in 1681 to statehood in 1787.
    ISBN 0-8239-5481-1
    1. Pennsylvania—History—Colonial period, ca. 1600–1775 Juvenile literature. 2. Pennsylvania—History—1775–1865 Juvenile literature. [1. Pennsylvania—History—Colonial period, ca. 1600–1775. 2. Pennsylvania—History—1775–1865.] I. Title. II. Series.
    F152 .W48 1999
    974.8'02—DC21   99-14962
                                                                                                 CIP

Manufactured in the United States of America

Contents

New Sweden

In the 1500s, **explorers** from Europe sailed across the ocean and came to a land they called the New World. Soon, many people came to settle there, in **colonies** that would later become the United States of America.

In the 1600s, people from Sweden, England, and the Netherlands moved to the area that is today known as Pennsylvania. They came to farm and trade with the local Indians. In 1643, Swedish colonists first settled on Tinicum Island, near today's Philadelphia. They called their settlement New Sweden. In 1655, soldiers from the Netherlands captured New Sweden and controlled it for nine years. The king of England's brother, the duke of York, took over the area in 1664. Finally, in 1681, King Charles II of England gave this land to an English Quaker named William Penn.

◀ *This historic painting shows King Charles II telling William Penn, who is dressed in black, that he will be given Pennsylvania.*

5

William Penn and the Quakers

King Charles II owed William Penn's family a lot of money. Instead of asking for the money, William Penn asked the king to pay back the **debt** with land in America. King Charles II gave Penn 28 million acres and named it Pennsylvania, which means "Penn's Woods" in Latin.

The Quakers' real name is the Society of Friends. They were called Quakers because of the way they prayed. They were said to shake, or "quake," because they prayed so long and hard.

William Penn was a Quaker. Quakers are a group of Christians who believe in peace, **equality**, and the importance of community. In the 1600s, Quakers were not free to worship in England. They could be put in jail or even killed. Penn had been in jail six times for his Quaker beliefs. He wanted to start a colony where people of all religions were free to worship.

This picture shows a Quaker woman and her hometown. ▶

Plans for Pennsylvania

In 1682, Penn and 100 Quakers sailed to America on a ship named *Welcome*. Penn decided to call the capital of the colony Philadelphia, which means "city of brotherly love" in Greek. He wanted the city to be beautiful, so he planned wide streets and large lots for homes.

Penn hoped that people in Pennsylvania could live in peace. He made a number of laws, called the Frame of Government, to govern the colony. Under his laws, a man **accused** of a crime had to have a **trial** with 12 **jurors**. All men who owned land could vote. Children had to be taught to read and write. Anyone who believed in the Christian God was free to worship in his own way. Penn wanted the laws in his colony to be more fair than the laws in England and in other colonies.

◄ *This picture of Philadelphia in the 1800s shows how quickly the city grew from its beginnings in 1682.*

Colonists and Indians

Few Colonial leaders in the 1600s thought about the rights of the Indians, who had lived on the land first. Colonists often took over land that already belonged to Native Americans. Penn wanted the colonists to treat the Indians fairly, and he wanted peace between Indians and colonists in Pennsylvania. In 1682, Penn met with Indians from the Delaware, Susquehannock, and Shawnee tribes. The Indians and colonists agreed to live together in peace and friendship. Delaware Chief Tamanend gave Penn a beaded **wampum** belt with a design of an Indian and a Quaker shaking hands. The meeting was the beginning of 70 years of friendship.

For his first piece of land, Penn paid 20 blankets, 20 kettles, 20 guns, 20 coats, 50 shirts, and a handful of pipes, scissors, shoes, combs, and knives.

William Penn told the colonists not to settle on any land until they had paid for it. Chief Tamanend and William Penn agreed that colonists and Indians should live in peace. ▶

Pennsylvania Starts to Grow

Penn sent advertisements to other countries to invite Quakers and people of other religions to come to Pennsylvania. By 1700, more than 4,000 settlers from all over Europe lived in Pennsylvania. People from some of the other American colonies also moved to Pennsylvania. A famous early American named Benjamin Franklin moved from Boston to Philadelphia in 1723.

Today, people say that Pennsylvania was one of the "Bread Colonies," the nickname given to colonies that grew a lot of wheat and other grains.

By this time, though, Pennsylvania had started to change. The English government wanted the colony to stop Catholics and Jews from voting, and some colonists owned **slaves**. Not all people in Pennsylvania were as free as Penn had hoped they would be.

◀ *Benjamin Franklin would later get France to help the colonies in their fight against England. He also helped to write the Declaration of Independence.*

War and Taxes

Between 1689 and 1763, England and France fought four wars over who would control America. To pay for soldiers, forts, and weapons, England began to tax the colonists. By the 1770s, the colonists were starting to get angry.

Before Washington D.C. became the capital of the United States, the capital was anywhere the Congress met. Philadelphia was the capital four times.

They thought it was unfair that they had to pay taxes to the English government when they were not allowed to vote in that government. When the colonists **protested** the taxes, England sent thousands of soldiers to the colonies. Benjamin Franklin suggested that men from all the colonies go to Philadelphia for a meeting called the First Continental Congress. Fifty-six men met in September 1774 to ask England to end the taxes.

This painting shows the signing of the Declaration of Independence during the First Continental Congress. ▶

Declaration of Independence

England did not listen to the First Continental Congress. Fighting soon broke out in Massachusetts between the British soldiers and the American **militia**. The Revolutionary War had begun. A Second Continental Congress met in Philadelphia. The Congress asked Thomas Jefferson, a colonist from Virginia, to write the Declaration of Independence to explain why the colonies should separate from England.

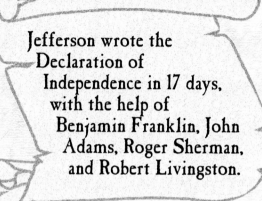

Jefferson wrote the Declaration of Independence in 17 days, with the help of Benjamin Franklin, John Adams, Roger Sherman, and Robert Livingston.

On July 4, 1776, the Congress approved the Declaration of Independence. Copies were sent to the 13 colonies that wanted to become states. When the declaration was read in Philadelphia, the bells rang all day and into the night.

◀ Thomas Jefferson, who is standing, gives Benjamin Franklin the Declaration of Independence so they can talk about what else needs to be included in it.

George Washington's Army

The Second Continental Congress asked a colonist named George Washington to lead the American army. In September 1777, Washington and his soldiers fought to keep the British out of Philadelphia. The British won this fight, called the Battle of Brandywine Creek. As the British moved in to capture Philadelphia, the Congress moved out.

After losing the Battle of Brandywine Creek, Washington decided to keep his army at Valley Forge, 25 miles west of Philadelphia, until spring. The 11,000 soldiers built hundreds of huts to live in. Half of the men had no shoes, and some days they had nothing to eat. George Washington's wife, Martha, and other soldiers' wives tried to take care of the sick soldiers, but 3,000 men died that winter at Valley Forge.

The winter at Valley Forge was cold and harsh. Soldiers did not have enough food to eat or clothes to wear. ▶

Help From France

Benjamin Franklin went to France to ask for help in the fight against the British. The French were angry about losing the war with England over land in America and agreed to help. The French sent **gunpowder**, soldiers, and ships to America. With the help of the French, the colonists won the war in 1781. The American colonies were free from England.

The war that the French lost to the British in 1763 was called the French and Indian War. After this, the British owned most of the land in North America.

To form a new government, **representatives** from all the states again traveled to Philadelphia. From May to September 1787, 55 men met at Independence Hall to write the Constitution. The Constitution explained how the new United States government would work.

Representatives from the 13 colonies signed the Constitution. The Constitution said that free men in the United States could vote to choose their leaders.

Pennsylvania's Proud History

On December 12, 1787, Pennsylvania became the second state to adopt the Constitution. The people of Pennsylvania are proud of their state's role in the history of our country. It was the home of William Penn, the First and Second Continental Congress, the Declaration of Independence, and the Constitution. Pennsylvania's nickname is the Keystone State, because so much of America's important early history happened there. A keystone holds other stones in a building together, just like Pennsylvania brought many colonies together to form the United States.

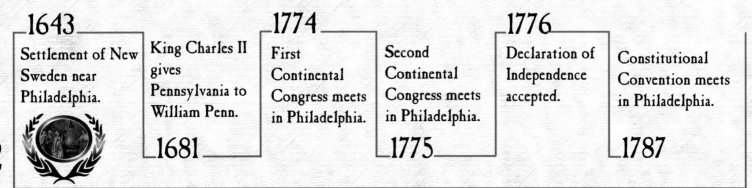

1643
Settlement of New Sweden near Philadelphia.

King Charles II gives Pennsylvania to William Penn.
1681

1774
First Continental Congress meets in Philadelphia.

Second Continental Congress meets in Philadelphia.
1775

1776
Declaration of Independence accepted.

Constitutional Convention meets in Philadelphia.
1787

Glossary

accused (uh-KYOOZD) When people say someone did or is something bad.

colonies (KAH-luh-neez) Areas in a new country where large groups of people move, who are still ruled by the leaders and laws of their old country.

debt (DET) When someone owes someone else something, usually money.

equality (ee-KWAH-lih-tee) When everyone has the same rights.

explorers (ik-SPLOR-urz) People who travel to different places to learn more about them.

gunpowder (GUN-pow-dur) A black powder that explodes in a gun and moves the bullet.

jurors (JOOR-uhrz) People who listen to all the facts at a trial and help decide whether the accused person is innocent or guilty.

militia (muh-LIH-shuh) A group of people who are trained to fight, but who are not in the army.

protested (PROH-tes-tid) Disagreed, or showed that you were upset about something.

representative (reh-prih-ZEN-tuh-tivs) Someone who presents the ideas, and stands up for the rights, of a certain group of people.

slaves (SLAYVz) People who are "owned" by another person and forced to work for him.

trial (TRYL) When a person goes to court and has his case presented to a judge or jury because he has been accused of a crime.

wampum (WAM-puhm) Beads made from sea shells.

Index

Web Sites:

You can learn more about Colonial Pennsylvania on the Internet. Check out this Web site:
http://www.state.pa.us/PA_Exec/Historical_Museum/colony.htm